ILLUSTRATED

ADDRESS BOOK

PUBLISHED BY VAN NOSTRAND REINHOLD COMPANY

COPYRIGHT © 1980 BY VAN NOSTRAND REINHOLD COMPANY INC.

ISBN 0–442–21257–7

McGUFFEY EDITIONS AND COLOPHON ARE TRADEMARKS OF
VAN NOSTRAND REINHOLD COMPANY INC.

ALL RIGHTS RESERVED.

PRINTED IN THE UNITED STATES OF AMERICA.

PUBLISHED IN 1980 BY McGUFFEY EDITIONS

VAN NOSTRAND REINHOLD COMPANY INC.

135 WEST 50TH STREET, NEW YORK, NEW YORK 10020.

PREFACE.

One hundred years ago the engraved illustrations found in this volume were familiar to every school child as pictures from the pages of *McGuffey's Eclectic Readers*. It was through this modest series of a primer and six graded readers, first published in 1836 and revised five times by 1911, that most young Americans of the nineteenth century first encountered Shakespeare, Milton, Wordsworth, Dickens, Poe, Homer, Milton, and other giants of literature. The lower readers and the primer taught the alphabet, penmanship, syllabification, inflection, spelling, and vocabulary, liberally laced with moral lessons to fortify the character at the same time as they developed the intellect.

The Eclectic Series was the brainchild of William Holmes McGuffey, born in 1800, the son of Scottish settlers in the frontier state of Pennsylvania. In a time when public schooling was nonexistent and the poor went uneducated, McGuffey struggled to attain a classical education and was rewarded for his efforts by a degree with honors from Washington College (Pennsylvania). Although ordained as a Presbyterian minister, he chose instead a distinguished career as professor of moral philosophy and president at both Cincinnati College and Ohio University at Athens. An enthusiastic supporter of the movement for public education, McGuffey had already begun compiling a school reader when he was approached by the Cincinnati textbook firm of Truman and Smith in 1835. The publisher had originally asked Catherine Beecher to prepare a text for them, but the sister of

Harriet Beecher Stowe doubted her ability to undertake such an ambitious task and recommended instead the family friend, William Holmes McGuffey.

In 1836, not much more than a year later, the earliest McGuffey Readers were issued: the slender, 72-page *First Reader* and the *Second Reader,* a full 164 pages long. They were bound in green paper-covered boards and the pages were roughly half the size of the volume you now hold in your hands. The 31-page *Primer,* step one of the graded texts, appeared the following year, along with the *Third* and *Fourth Readers,* 165 and 324 pages respectively and printed on a somewhat larger page than the original two readers.

Although McGuffey's Readers were by no means the first books of their kind, they were distinguished by (and undoubtedly owed their phenomenal success to) their new approach to learning. Unlike the Puritan *New England Primer* and such works as Murray's *English* and *American Readers,* the *Goodrich School Readers,* and the *Child's Instructer and Moral Primer,* the Mc-Guffeys abandoned religious themes rendered in awesome and frequently terrifying terms in favor of selections of literary merit designed to suit the age level and interest of the students. This is not to say the lessons were without moral content; rather, Dr. McGuffey forswore hellfire and opted instead for the promotion by example of such virtues as integrity, honesty, patriotism, filial duty, industry, temperance, courage, and politeness.

The combination worked. By 1920, sales of over 125 million were reported by the publisher, by then The American Book Company. Although a search of the nation's attics would undoubtedly yield a portion of those many millions, the readers are now considered collectors' items and the best of them are housed in museums and private collections, notably the Henry Ford Collection in the Edison Institute Museum in Dearborn, Michigan, and the McGuffey Museum in Oxford, Ohio.

As the readers gained popularity, an attempt was made to keep them abreast of changes in the educational and social climate. With the help of a Dr. Pinneo, of Yale University, W. H. Mc-Guffey enlarged and redesigned the first four readers, which were issued in 1844 as "Newly Revised." In that same year, the

Fifth Reader was published, though it was prepared by another McGuffey, William Holmes' younger brother, Alexander. The year 1853 saw the publication of the *Sixth Reader,* the last in the series.

From the outset, W. H. McGuffey determined that the books should be suitably illustrated. He knew well that pictures could spur interest as well as aid in pedagogy. As the Preface to an 1881 printing of the *Primer* stated: "Illustrations of the best character have been freely supplied, and the skilled teacher will be able to use them to great advantage." Teachers of the *First Reader* were informed that "Many of these engravings will serve admirably as the basis for oral lessons in language."

McGuffey's innovation was in choosing artwork with direct appeal for children. Rather than the dreary and forbidding illustrations of classical and biblical subjects, he used pictures of children pursuing the activities of childhood. Toys and pets were the order of the day, dogs being a particular favorite. In fact, of 153 engravings in the *First Reader,* 21 feature dogs, and in the several editions, the number of dog pictures approaches 200. Animals of all sorts—as exotic as lions in jungle settings and elephants in caravans, as common as goats drawing carts and cats trapping rats—decorated the pages. Children at play, in all seasons, at work, and at mischief, could be found throughout, with only the occasional grown-up to add a sober note to the scene.

In the first edition, McGuffey used no original art at all, borrowing instead English school book illustrations. To the 1844 revision he added some original engravings, and by 1853 all the artwork was covered by the publisher's copyright. The edition of 1863 employed for the first time wood engravings executed by a master engraver, E. J. Whitney, to whom due credit was given. The edition of 1879 featured the work of artists of national reputation and steel engravings signed both by artist and engraver. As the Preface to the *Second Reader* of that period expressed it: "Great care has been taken to have the illustrations worthy of the reputation McGUFFEY'S READERS have attained, and some of the foremost designers of this country have contributed to the embellishment of the book."

AX.
ax.

Aa

NAME.

ADDRESS.

TELEPHONE.

NAME.

ADDRESS.

TELEPHONE.

NAME.

ADDRESS.

TELEPHONE.

NAME.

ADDRESS.

TELEPHONE.

NAME.

ADDRESS.

TELEPHONE.

A a

NAME.

ADDRESS.

TELEPHONE.

NAME.

ADDRESS.

TELEPHONE.

NAME.

ADDRESS.

TELEPHONE.

NAME.

ADDRESS.

TELEPHONE.

NAME.

ADDRESS.

TELEPHONE.

NAME.

ADDRESS.

TELEPHONE.

Aa

NAME.

ADDRESS.

TELEPHONE.

NAME.

ADDRESS.

TELEPHONE.

Aa

NAME.
_____

ADDRESS.
_____
              TELEPHONE.
_____

NAME.
_____

ADDRESS.
_____
              TELEPHONE.
_____

NAME.
_____

ADDRESS.
_____
              TELEPHONE.
_____

NAME.
_____

ADDRESS.
_____
              TELEPHONE.
_____

NAME.
_____

ADDRESS.
_____
              TELEPHONE.
_____

NAME.
_____

ADDRESS.
_____
              TELEPHONE.
_____

NAME.

ADDRESS.

TELEPHONE.

NAME.

ADDRESS.

TELEPHONE.

NAME.

ADDRESS.

TELEPHONE.

NAME.

ADDRESS.

TELEPHONE.

Bb

NAME.

ADDRESS.

TELEPHONE.

NAME.

ADDRESS.

TELEPHONE.

THE BEE.

BOX.
box.

Bb

NAME.

ADDRESS.

TELEPHONE.

NAME.

ADDRESS.

TELEPHONE.

NAME.

ADDRESS.

TELEPHONE.

NAME.

ADDRESS.

TELEPHONE.

NAME.

ADDRESS.

TELEPHONE.

Bb

NAME.

ADDRESS.

TELEPHONE.

NAME.

ADDRESS.

TELEPHONE.

NAME.

ADDRESS.

TELEPHONE.

NAME.

ADDRESS.

TELEPHONE.

NAME.

ADDRESS.

TELEPHONE.

NAME.

ADDRESS.

TELEPHONE.

Bb

MARY'S DIME.

Bb

NAME.
_____

ADDRESS.
_____

TELEPHONE.
_____

NAME.
_____

ADDRESS.
_____

TELEPHONE.
_____

NAME.
_____

ADDRESS.
_____

TELEPHONE.
_____

NAME.
_____

ADDRESS.
_____

TELEPHONE.
_____

NAME.
_____

ADDRESS.
_____

TELEPHONE.
_____

NAME.
_____

ADDRESS.
_____

TELEPHONE.
_____

Bb

NAME.

ADDRESS.

TELEPHONE.

NAME.

ADDRESS.

TELEPHONE.

NAME.

ADDRESS.

TELEPHONE.

NAME.

ADDRESS.

TELEPHONE.

| CAT. |
| cat. |

C c

NAME.

ADDRESS.

TELEPHONE.

NAME.

ADDRESS.

TELEPHONE.

NAME.

ADDRESS.

TELEPHONE.

NAME.

ADDRESS.

TELEPHONE.

NAME.

ADDRESS.

TELEPHONE.

Cc

NAME.

ADDRESS.

TELEPHONE.

NAME.

ADDRESS.

TELEPHONE.

NAME.

ADDRESS.

TELEPHONE.

NAME.

ADDRESS.

TELEPHONE.

NAME.

ADDRESS.

TELEPHONE.

NAME.

ADDRESS.

TELEPHONE.

Cc

NAME.

ADDRESS.

TELEPHONE.

NAME.

ADDRESS.

TELEPHONE.

Cc

NAME.

ADDRESS.

TELEPHONE.

NAME.

ADDRESS.

TELEPHONE.

NAME.

ADDRESS.

TELEPHONE.

NAME.

ADDRESS.

TELEPHONE.

NAME.

ADDRESS.

TELEPHONE.

NAME.

ADDRESS.

TELEPHONE.

Cc

NAME.

ADDRESS.

TELEPHONE.

NAME.

ADDRESS.

TELEPHONE.

NAME.

ADDRESS.

TELEPHONE.

NAME.

ADDRESS.

TELEPHONE.

D d

NAME.

ADDRESS.

TELEPHONE.

NAME.

ADDRESS.

TELEPHONE.

DOG.
dog.

Dd

NAME.

ADDRESS.

TELEPHONE.

NAME.

ADDRESS.

TELEPHONE.

NAME.

ADDRESS.

TELEPHONE.

NAME.

ADDRESS.

TELEPHONE.

NAME.

ADDRESS.

TELEPHONE.

Dd

NAME.

ADDRESS.

TELEPHONE.

NAME.

ADDRESS.

TELEPHONE.

NAME.

ADDRESS.

TELEPHONE.

NAME.

ADDRESS.

TELEPHONE.

NAME.

ADDRESS.

TELEPHONE.

NAME.

ADDRESS.

TELEPHONE.

Dd

NAME.

ADDRESS.

TELEPHONE.

NAME.

ADDRESS.

TELEPHONE.

NAME.

ADDRESS.

TELEPHONE.

D d

NAME.

ADDRESS.

TELEPHONE.

NAME.

ADDRESS.

TELEPHONE.

NAME.

ADDRESS.

TELEPHONE.

NAME.

ADDRESS.

TELEPHONE.

NAME.

ADDRESS.

TELEPHONE.

NAME.

ADDRESS.

TELEPHONE.

THE CHICKADEE.

NAME.

ADDRESS.

        TELEPHONE.

NAME.

ADDRESS.

        TELEPHONE.

NAME.

ADDRESS.

        TELEPHONE.

NAME.

ADDRESS.

TELEPHONE.

ELK.
elk.

Ee

NAME.

ADDRESS.

TELEPHONE.

NAME.

ADDRESS.

TELEPHONE.

NAME.

ADDRESS.

TELEPHONE.

NAME.

ADDRESS.

TELEPHONE.

NAME.

ADDRESS.

TELEPHONE.

Ee

NAME.

ADDRESS.

TELEPHONE.

NAME.

ADDRESS.

TELEPHONE.

NAME.

ADDRESS.

TELEPHONE.

NAME.

ADDRESS.

TELEPHONE.

NAME.

ADDRESS.

TELEPHONE.

NAME.

ADDRESS.

TELEPHONE.

Ee

NAME.

ADDRESS.

TELEPHONE.

NAME.

ADDRESS.

TELEPHONE.

Ee

NAME.

ADDRESS.

TELEPHONE.

NAME.

ADDRESS.

TELEPHONE.

NAME.

ADDRESS.

TELEPHONE.

Ee

NAME.

ADDRESS.

TELEPHONE.

NAME.

ADDRESS.

TELEPHONE.

NAME.

ADDRESS.

TELEPHONE.

NAME.

ADDRESS.

TELEPHONE.

NAME.

ADDRESS.

TELEPHONE.

NAME.

ADDRESS.

TELEPHONE.

F f

NAME.

ADDRESS.

TELEPHONE.

NAME.

ADDRESS.

TELEPHONE.

FAN.
fan.

Ff

NAME.

ADDRESS.

TELEPHONE.

NAME.

ADDRESS.

TELEPHONE.

NAME.

ADDRESS.

TELEPHONE.

NAME.

ADDRESS.

TELEPHONE.

NAME.

ADDRESS.

TELEPHONE.

F f

NAME.

ADDRESS.

TELEPHONE.

NAME.

ADDRESS.

TELEPHONE.

NAME.

ADDRESS.

TELEPHONE.

NAME.

ADDRESS.

TELEPHONE.

NAME.

ADDRESS.

TELEPHONE.

NAME.

ADDRESS.

TELEPHONE.

CASTLE-BUILDING.

NAME.

ADDRESS.

TELEPHONE.

NAME.

ADDRESS.

TELEPHONE.

NAME.

ADDRESS.

TELEPHONE.

F f

NAME.

ADDRESS.

TELEPHONE.

NAME.

ADDRESS.

TELEPHONE.

NAME.

ADDRESS.

TELEPHONE.

NAME.

ADDRESS.

TELEPHONE.

NAME.

ADDRESS.

TELEPHONE.

NAME.

ADDRESS.

TELEPHONE.

F f

NAME.

ADDRESS.

TELEPHONE.

NAME.

ADDRESS.

TELEPHONE.

NAME.

ADDRESS.

TELEPHONE.

NAME.

ADDRESS.

TELEPHONE.

YOUNG SOLDIERS.

We charged upon a flock of geese,
   And put them all to flight—
Except one sturdy gander
   That thought to show us fight.

NAME.

ADDRESS.

             TELEPHONE.

NAME.

ADDRESS.

             TELEPHONE.

GIRL.
girl.

G g

NAME.

ADDRESS.

TELEPHONE.

NAME.

ADDRESS.

TELEPHONE.

NAME.

ADDRESS.

TELEPHONE.

NAME.

ADDRESS.

TELEPHONE.

NAME.

ADDRESS.

TELEPHONE.

G g

NAME.

ADDRESS.

TELEPHONE.

NAME.

ADDRESS.

TELEPHONE.

NAME.

ADDRESS.

TELEPHONE.

NAME.

ADDRESS.

TELEPHONE.

NAME.

ADDRESS.

TELEPHONE.

NAME.

ADDRESS.

TELEPHONE.

Gg

NAME.

ADDRESS.

TELEPHONE.

NAME.

ADDRESS.

TELEPHONE.

Gg

NAME.

ADDRESS.

TELEPHONE.

NAME.

ADDRESS.

TELEPHONE.

NAME.

ADDRESS.

TELEPHONE.

NAME.

ADDRESS.

TELEPHONE.

NAME.

ADDRESS.

TELEPHONE.

NAME.

ADDRESS.

TELEPHONE.

Gg

NAME.

ADDRESS.

TELEPHONE.

NAME.

ADDRESS.

TELEPHONE.

NAME.

ADDRESS.

TELEPHONE.

NAME.

ADDRESS.

TELEPHONE.

H h

HEN.
hen.

Hh

NAME.

ADDRESS.

TELEPHONE.

NAME.

ADDRESS.

TELEPHONE.

NAME.

ADDRESS.

TELEPHONE.

NAME.

ADDRESS.

TELEPHONE.

NAME.

ADDRESS.

TELEPHONE.

NAME.

ADDRESS.

TELEPHONE.

NAME.

ADDRESS.

TELEPHONE.

NAME.

ADDRESS.

TELEPHONE.

H h

NAME.

ADDRESS.

TELEPHONE.

NAME.

ADDRESS.

TELEPHONE.

NAME.

ADDRESS.

TELEPHONE.

NAME.

ADDRESS.

TELEPHONE.

NAME.

ADDRESS.

TELEPHONE.

NAME.

ADDRESS.

TELEPHONE.

H h

NAME.

ADDRESS.

TELEPHONE.

NAME.

ADDRESS.

TELEPHONE.

NAME.

ADDRESS.

TELEPHONE.

NAME.

ADDRESS.

TELEPHONE.

NAME.

ADDRESS.

TELEPHONE.

NAME.

ADDRESS.

TELEPHONE.

H h

NAME.

ADDRESS.

TELEPHONE.

NAME.

ADDRESS.

TELEPHONE.

NAME.

ADDRESS.

TELEPHONE.

NAME.

ADDRESS.

TELEPHONE.

WM. E. PARKER

I i

HARRY AND ANNIE.

INK.
ink.

I i

NAME.

ADDRESS.

 TELEPHONE.

NAME.

ADDRESS.

 TELEPHONE.

NAME.

ADDRESS.

 TELEPHONE.

NAME.

ADDRESS.

 TELEPHONE.

NAME.

ADDRESS.

 TELEPHONE.

I i

NAME.

ADDRESS.

TELEPHONE.

NAME.

ADDRESS.

TELEPHONE.

NAME.

ADDRESS.

TELEPHONE.

NAME.

ADDRESS.

TELEPHONE.

NAME.

ADDRESS.

TELEPHONE.

NAME.

ADDRESS.

TELEPHONE.

nīne   mous'ie

frō   frŏl'ie

bĭt   slĭpped

spīed

ᴄrōw

tēeth

pẽarl

ūşed

KITTY AND MOUSIE.

NAME.

ADDRESS.

TELEPHONE.

NAME.

ADDRESS.

TELEPHONE.

NAME.

ADDRESS.

TELEPHONE.

I i

NAME.

ADDRESS.

TELEPHONE.

NAME.

ADDRESS.

TELEPHONE.

NAME.

ADDRESS.

TELEPHONE.

THE EARLY HOME OF A HORSE.

I i

NAME.

ADDRESS.

TELEPHONE.

NAME.

ADDRESS.

TELEPHONE.

NAME.

ADDRESS.

TELEPHONE.

NAME.

ADDRESS.

TELEPHONE.

NAME.

ADDRESS.

TELEPHONE.

NAME.

ADDRESS.

TELEPHONE.

NAME.

ADDRESS.

TELEPHONE.

NAME.

ADDRESS.

TELEPHONE.

JUG.
jug.

J j

NAME.

ADDRESS.

TELEPHONE.

NAME.

ADDRESS.

TELEPHONE.

NAME.

ADDRESS.

TELEPHONE.

NAME.

ADDRESS.

TELEPHONE.

NAME.

ADDRESS.

TELEPHONE.

J j

NAME.

ADDRESS.

TELEPHONE.

NAME.

ADDRESS.

TELEPHONE.

NAME.

ADDRESS.

TELEPHONE.

NAME.

ADDRESS.

TELEPHONE.

NAME.

ADDRESS.

TELEPHONE.

NAME.

ADDRESS.

TELEPHONE.

J j

THE BEAVER.

J j

J j

NAME.

ADDRESS.

TELEPHONE.

NAME.

ADDRESS.

TELEPHONE.

NAME.

ADDRESS.

TELEPHONE.

NAME.

ADDRESS.

TELEPHONE.

NAME.

ADDRESS.

TELEPHONE.

NAME.

ADDRESS.

TELEPHONE.

K k

NAME.

ADDRESS.

TELEPHONE.

NAME.

ADDRESS.

TELEPHONE.

KID.
kid.

K k

NAME.

ADDRESS.

TELEPHONE.

NAME.

ADDRESS.

TELEPHONE.

NAME.

ADDRESS.

TELEPHONE.

NAME.

ADDRESS.

TELEPHONE.

NAME.

ADDRESS.

TELEPHONE.

K k

NAME.

ADDRESS.

TELEPHONE.

NAME.

ADDRESS.

TELEPHONE.

NAME.

ADDRESS.

TELEPHONE.

NAME.

ADDRESS.

TELEPHONE.

NAME.

ADDRESS.

TELEPHONE.

NAME.

ADDRESS.

TELEPHONE.

K k

NAME.

ADDRESS.

TELEPHONE.

NAME.

ADDRESS.

TELEPHONE.

NAME.

ADDRESS.

TELEPHONE.

NAME.

ADDRESS.

TELEPHONE.

NAME.

ADDRESS.

TELEPHONE.

NAME.

ADDRESS.

TELEPHONE.

K k

NAME.

ADDRESS.

TELEPHONE.

NAME.

ADDRESS.

TELEPHONE.

NAME.

ADDRESS.

TELEPHONE.

NAME.

ADDRESS.

TELEPHONE.

NAME.

ADDRESS.

TELEPHONE.

NAME.

ADDRESS.

TELEPHONE.

Ll

THE BIRDS SET FREE.

NAME.

ADDRESS.

TELEPHONE.

NAME.

ADDRESS.

TELEPHONE.

NAME.

ADDRESS.

TELEPHONE.

NAME.

ADDRESS.

TELEPHONE.

NAME.

ADDRESS.

TELEPHONE.

Ll

NAME.

ADDRESS.

TELEPHONE.

NAME.

ADDRESS.

TELEPHONE.

NAME.

ADDRESS.

TELEPHONE.

NAME.

ADDRESS.

TELEPHONE.

NAME.

ADDRESS.

TELEPHONE.

NAME.

ADDRESS.

TELEPHONE.

NAME.

ADDRESS.

TELEPHONE.

NAME.

ADDRESS.

TELEPHONE.

NAME.

ADDRESS.

TELEPHONE.

THE PERT CHICKEN.

NAME.

ADDRESS.

TELEPHONE.

NAME.

ADDRESS.

TELEPHONE.

NAME.

ADDRESS.

TELEPHONE.

Ll

NAME.

ADDRESS.

TELEPHONE.

NAME.

ADDRESS.

TELEPHONE.

NAME.

ADDRESS.

TELEPHONE.

NAME.

ADDRESS.

TELEPHONE.

NAME.

ADDRESS.

TELEPHONE.

NAME.

ADDRESS.

TELEPHONE.

MAN.
man.
Mm

NAME.

ADDRESS.

TELEPHONE.

NAME.

ADDRESS.

TELEPHONE.

NAME.

ADDRESS.

TELEPHONE.

NAME.

ADDRESS.

TELEPHONE.

NAME.

ADDRESS.

TELEPHONE.

M m

NAME.

ADDRESS.

TELEPHONE.

NAME.

ADDRESS.

TELEPHONE.

NAME.

ADDRESS.

TELEPHONE.

NAME.

ADDRESS.

TELEPHONE.

NAME.

ADDRESS.

TELEPHONE.

NAME.

ADDRESS.

TELEPHONE.

M m

NAME.

ADDRESS.

TELEPHONE.

NAME.

ADDRESS.

TELEPHONE.

NAME.

ADDRESS.

TELEPHONE.

M m

NAME.

ADDRESS.

TELEPHONE.

NAME.

ADDRESS.

TELEPHONE.

NAME.

ADDRESS.

TELEPHONE.

NAME.

ADDRESS.

TELEPHONE.

NAME.

ADDRESS.

TELEPHONE.

NAME.

ADDRESS.

TELEPHONE.

NAME.

ADDRESS.

TELEPHONE.

NAME.

ADDRESS.

TELEPHONE.

N n

NAME.

ADDRESS.

TELEPHONE.

NAME.

ADDRESS.

TELEPHONE.

NUT.
nut.

N n

NAME.

ADDRESS.

TELEPHONE.

NAME.

ADDRESS.

TELEPHONE.

NAME.

ADDRESS.

TELEPHONE.

NAME.

ADDRESS.

TELEPHONE.

NAME.

ADDRESS.

TELEPHONE.

N n

NAME.

ADDRESS.

TELEPHONE.

NAME.

ADDRESS.

TELEPHONE.

NAME.

ADDRESS.

TELEPHONE.

NAME.

ADDRESS.

TELEPHONE.

NAME.

ADDRESS.

TELEPHONE.

NAME.

ADDRESS.

TELEPHONE.

NAME.

ADDRESS.

TELEPHONE.

NAME.

ADDRESS.

TELEPHONE.

NAME.

ADDRESS.

TELEPHONE.

NAME.

ADDRESS.

TELEPHONE.

N n

NAME.

ADDRESS.

TELEPHONE.

NAME.

ADDRESS.

TELEPHONE.

NAME.

ADDRESS.

TELEPHONE.

N n

NAME.

ADDRESS.

TELEPHONE.

NAME.

ADDRESS.

TELEPHONE.

NAME.

ADDRESS.

TELEPHONE.

NAME.

ADDRESS.

TELEPHONE.

NAME.

ADDRESS.

TELEPHONE.

NAME.

ADDRESS.

TELEPHONE.

NAME.

ADDRESS.

TELEPHONE.

NAME.

ADDRESS.

TELEPHONE.

NAME.

ADDRESS.

TELEPHONE.

OX.
ox.

O o

NAME.

ADDRESS.

TELEPHONE.

NAME.

ADDRESS.

TELEPHONE.

NAME.

ADDRESS.

TELEPHONE.

NAME.

ADDRESS.

TELEPHONE.

NAME.

ADDRESS.

TELEPHONE.

Oo

NAME.

ADDRESS.

TELEPHONE.

NAME.

ADDRESS.

TELEPHONE.

NAME.

ADDRESS.

TELEPHONE.

NAME.

ADDRESS.

TELEPHONE.

NAME.

ADDRESS.

TELEPHONE.

NAME.

ADDRESS.

TELEPHONE.

Oo

NAME.

ADDRESS.

TELEPHONE.

NAME.

ADDRESS.

TELEPHONE.

NAME.

ADDRESS.

                TELEPHONE.

NAME.

ADDRESS.

                TELEPHONE.

NAME.

ADDRESS.

                TELEPHONE.

NAME.

ADDRESS.

                TELEPHONE.

Oo

NAME.

ADDRESS.

TELEPHONE.

NAME.

ADDRESS.

TELEPHONE.

NAME.

ADDRESS.

TELEPHONE.

NAME.

ADDRESS.

TELEPHONE.

NAME.

ADDRESS.

TELEPHONE.

NAME.

ADDRESS.

TELEPHONE.

Pp

COASTING DOWN THE HILL.

PIG.
pig.

Pp

NAME.

ADDRESS.

TELEPHONE.

NAME.

ADDRESS.

TELEPHONE.

NAME.

ADDRESS.

TELEPHONE.

NAME.

ADDRESS.

TELEPHONE.

NAME.

ADDRESS.

TELEPHONE.

Pp

NAME.

ADDRESS.

TELEPHONE.

NAME.

ADDRESS.

TELEPHONE.

NAME.

ADDRESS.

TELEPHONE.

NAME.

ADDRESS.

TELEPHONE.

NAME.

ADDRESS.

TELEPHONE.

NAME.

ADDRESS.

TELEPHONE.

NAME.

ADDRESS.

TELEPHONE.

NAME.

ADDRESS.

TELEPHONE.

NAME.

ADDRESS.

TELEPHONE.

Pp

NAME.

ADDRESS.

TELEPHONE.

NAME.

ADDRESS.

TELEPHONE.

NAME.

ADDRESS.

TELEPHONE.

NAME.

ADDRESS.

TELEPHONE.

NAME.

ADDRESS.

TELEPHONE.

NAME.

ADDRESS.

TELEPHONE.

NAME.

ADDRESS.

TELEPHONE.

NAME.

ADDRESS.

TELEPHONE.

Q q

NAME.

ADDRESS.

TELEPHONE.

NAME.

ADDRESS.

TELEPHONE.

QUAIL.
quail.

Q q

NAME.

ADDRESS.

TELEPHONE.

NAME.

ADDRESS.

TELEPHONE.

NAME.

ADDRESS.

TELEPHONE.

NAME.

ADDRESS.

TELEPHONE.

NAME.

ADDRESS.

TELEPHONE.

Q q

NAME.

ADDRESS.

TELEPHONE.

NAME.

ADDRESS.

TELEPHONE.

NAME.

ADDRESS.

TELEPHONE.

NAME.

ADDRESS.

TELEPHONE.

NAME.

ADDRESS.

TELEPHONE.

NAME.

ADDRESS.

TELEPHONE.

Q q

NAME.

ADDRESS.

TELEPHONE.

NAME.

ADDRESS.

TELEPHONE.

NAME.

ADDRESS.

TELEPHONE.

EVENING AT HOME.

NAME.

ADDRESS.

TELEPHONE.

NAME.

ADDRESS.

TELEPHONE.

Q q

NAME.

ADDRESS.

        TELEPHONE.

NAME.

ADDRESS.

        TELEPHONE.

NAME.

ADDRESS.

        TELEPHONE.

NAME.

ADDRESS.

RAT.		
rat.	# R r	

NAME.

ADDRESS.

TELEPHONE.

NAME.

ADDRESS.

TELEPHONE.

NAME.

ADDRESS.

TELEPHONE.

NAME.

ADDRESS.

TELEPHONE.

NAME.

ADDRESS.

TELEPHONE.

R r

NAME.

ADDRESS.

TELEPHONE.

NAME.

ADDRESS.

TELEPHONE.

NAME.

ADDRESS.

TELEPHONE.

NAME.

ADDRESS.

TELEPHONE.

NAME.

ADDRESS.

TELEPHONE.

NAME.

ADDRESS.

TELEPHONE.

—∘∘⦂⦂∘∘—

THE VILLAGE GREEN.

On the cheerful village green,
    Scattered round with houses neat,
All the boys and girls are seen,
    Playing there with busy feet.

NAME.

ADDRESS.

          TELEPHONE.

NAME.

ADDRESS.

          TELEPHONE.

NAME.

ADDRESS.

          TELEPHONE.

Rr

NAME.

ADDRESS.

TELEPHONE.

NAME.

ADDRESS.

TELEPHONE.

NAME.

ADDRESS.

TELEPHONE.

BESSIE.

R r

NAME.

ADDRESS.

TELEPHONE.

NAME.

ADDRESS.

TELEPHONE.

NAME.

ADDRESS.

TELEPHONE.

NAME.

ADDRESS.

TELEPHONE.

NAME.

ADDRESS.

TELEPHONE.

NAME.

ADDRESS.

TELEPHONE.

S s

NAME.

ADDRESS.

TELEPHONE.

NAME.

ADDRESS.

TELEPHONE.

NAME.

ADDRESS.

TELEPHONE.

PRETTY IS THAT PRETTY DOES.

SUN.
sun.

S s

NAME.

ADDRESS.

TELEPHONE.

NAME.

ADDRESS.

TELEPHONE.

NAME.

ADDRESS.

TELEPHONE.

NAME.

ADDRESS.

TELEPHONE.

NAME.

ADDRESS.

TELEPHONE.

S s

NAME.

ADDRESS.

TELEPHONE.

NAME.

ADDRESS.

TELEPHONE.

NAME.

ADDRESS.

TELEPHONE.

NAME.

ADDRESS.

TELEPHONE.

NAME.

ADDRESS.

TELEPHONE.

NAME.

ADDRESS.

TELEPHONE.

S s

SHEEP-SHEARING.

im mē′di ate ly   en ꞓoun′tered

ehăr′ae ter   pre pâred′

squēal   pŏl′i çy

snăpped   prowl′ing

shŭnned   doŭ′ble

quĭllṣ   ĭn′seet

tĕr′ri bly   de vour′

erĕv′iç eṣ   es eāpe′

frāme′wõrk   nīght′mâre   dis ḡŭst′ing   quạd′rụ ped

BATS.

NAME.

ADDRESS.

           TELEPHONE.

NAME.

ADDRESS.

           TELEPHONE.

NAME.

ADDRESS.

           TELEPHONE.

S s

NAME.

ADDRESS.

TELEPHONE.

NAME.

ADDRESS.

TELEPHONE.

NAME.

ADDRESS.

TELEPHONE.

NAME.

ADDRESS.

TELEPHONE.

NAME.

ADDRESS.

TELEPHONE.

NAME.

ADDRESS.

TELEPHONE.

THE YOUNG TEACHER.

NAME.

ADDRESS.

TELEPHONE.

NAME.

ADDRESS.

TELEPHONE.

NAME.

ADDRESS.

TELEPHONE.

TUB.
tub.

Tt

NAME.

ADDRESS.

TELEPHONE.

NAME.

ADDRESS.

TELEPHONE.

NAME.

ADDRESS.

TELEPHONE.

NAME.

ADDRESS.

TELEPHONE.

NAME.

ADDRESS.

TELEPHONE.

Tt

NAME.

ADDRESS.

TELEPHONE.

NAME.

ADDRESS.

TELEPHONE.

NAME.

ADDRESS.

TELEPHONE.

NAME.

ADDRESS.

TELEPHONE.

NAME.

ADDRESS.

TELEPHONE.

NAME.

ADDRESS.

TELEPHONE.

Tt

NAME.

ADDRESS.

TELEPHONE.

NAME.

ADDRESS.

TELEPHONE.

NAME.

ADDRESS.

TELEPHONE.

NAME.

ADDRESS.

TELEPHONE.

NAME.

ADDRESS.

TELEPHONE.

Tt

NAME.

ADDRESS.

TELEPHONE.

NAME.

ADDRESS.

TELEPHONE.

NAME.

ADDRESS.

TELEPHONE.

URN.
urn.

U u

NAME.

ADDRESS.

TELEPHONE.

NAME.

ADDRESS.

TELEPHONE.

NAME.

ADDRESS.

TELEPHONE.

NAME.

ADDRESS.

TELEPHONE.

NAME.

ADDRESS.

TELEPHONE.

LEON CUIPON.

NAME.

ADDRESS.

TELEPHONE.

NAME.

ADDRESS.

TELEPHONE.

NAME.

ADDRESS.

TELEPHONE.

NAME.

ADDRESS.

TELEPHONE.

NAME.

ADDRESS.

TELEPHONE.

U u

NAME.

ADDRESS.

TELEPHONE.

NAME.

ADDRESS.

TELEPHONE.

NAME.

ADDRESS.

TELEPHONE.

U u

NAME.

ADDRESS.

TELEPHONE.

NAME.

ADDRESS.

TELEPHONE.

NAME.

ADDRESS.

TELEPHONE.

NAME.

ADDRESS.

TELEPHONE.

NAME.

ADDRESS.

TELEPHONE.

NAME.

ADDRESS.

TELEPHONE.

U u

NAME.

ADDRESS.

TELEPHONE.

NAME.

ADDRESS.

TELEPHONE.

NAME.

ADDRESS.

TELEPHONE.

COURAGE AND COWARDICE.

NAME.

ADDRESS.

TELEPHONE.

NAME.

ADDRESS.

TELEPHONE.

NAME.

ADDRESS.

TELEPHONE.

VINE.
vine.

Vv

NAME.

ADDRESS.

TELEPHONE.

NAME.

ADDRESS.

TELEPHONE.

NAME.

ADDRESS.

TELEPHONE.

NAME.

ADDRESS.

TELEPHONE.

NAME.

ADDRESS.

TELEPHONE.

Vv

NAME.

ADDRESS.

TELEPHONE.

NAME.

ADDRESS.

TELEPHONE.

NAME.

ADDRESS.

TELEPHONE.

NAME.

ADDRESS.

TELEPHONE.

NAME.

ADDRESS.

TELEPHONE.

NAME.

ADDRESS.

TELEPHONE.

V v

NAME.

ADDRESS.

TELEPHONE.

NAME.

ADDRESS.

TELEPHONE.

NAME.

ADDRESS.

TELEPHONE.

V v

NAME.

ADDRESS.

TELEPHONE.

NAME.

ADDRESS.

TELEPHONE.

NAME.

ADDRESS.

TELEPHONE.

Vv

NAME.

ADDRESS.

TELEPHONE.

NAME.

ADDRESS.

TELEPHONE.

NAME.

ADDRESS.

TELEPHONE.

NAME.

ADDRESS.

TELEPHONE.

NAME.

ADDRESS.

TELEPHONE.

NAME.

ADDRESS.

TELEPHONE.

NAME.

ADDRESS.

                       TELEPHONE.

NAME.

ADDRESS.

                       TELEPHONE.

NAME.

ADDRESS.

                       TELEPHONE.

WASP.
wasp.

NAME.

ADDRESS.

          TELEPHONE.

NAME.

ADDRESS.

          TELEPHONE.

NAME.

ADDRESS.

          TELEPHONE.

NAME.

ADDRESS.

          TELEPHONE.

NAME.

ADDRESS.

          TELEPHONE.

Ww

măn   eăp

lăd   săt

W w

NAME.

ADDRESS.

TELEPHONE.

NAME.

ADDRESS.

TELEPHONE.

NAME.

ADDRESS.

TELEPHONE.

NAME.

ADDRESS.

TELEPHONE.

NAME.

ADDRESS.

TELEPHONE.

NAME.

ADDRESS.

TELEPHONE.

W w

NAME.

ADDRESS.

TELEPHONE.

NAME.

ADDRESS.

TELEPHONE.

NAME.

ADDRESS.

TELEPHONE.

NAME.

ADDRESS.

TELEPHONE.

NAME.

ADDRESS.

TELEPHONE.

NAME.

ADDRESS.

TELEPHONE.

W w

X x

NAME.

ADDRESS.

TELEPHONE.

NAME.

ADDRESS.

TELEPHONE.

NAME.

ADDRESS.

TELEPHONE.

EX.
ex.

NAME.

ADDRESS.

TELEPHONE.

NAME.

ADDRESS.

TELEPHONE.

NAME.

ADDRESS.

TELEPHONE.

NAME.

ADDRESS.

TELEPHONE.

NAME.

ADDRESS.

TELEPHONE.

X x

NAME.

ADDRESS.

TELEPHONE.

NAME.

ADDRESS.

TELEPHONE.

NAME.

ADDRESS.

TELEPHONE.

NAME.

ADDRESS.

TELEPHONE.

NAME.

ADDRESS.

TELEPHONE.

NAME.

ADDRESS.

TELEPHONE.

NAME.

ADDRESS.

TELEPHONE.

Y y

NAME.

ADDRESS.

TELEPHONE.

NAME.

ADDRESS.

TELEPHONE.

YOKE.
yoke.

Y y

NAME.

ADDRESS.

TELEPHONE.

NAME.

ADDRESS.

TELEPHONE.

NAME.

ADDRESS.

TELEPHONE.

NAME.

ADDRESS.

TELEPHONE.

NAME.

ADDRESS.

TELEPHONE.

Y y

NAME.

ADDRESS.

TELEPHONE.

NAME.

ADDRESS.

TELEPHONE.

NAME.

ADDRESS.

TELEPHONE.

NAME.

ADDRESS.

TELEPHONE.

NAME.

ADDRESS.

TELEPHONE.

NAME.

ADDRESS.

TELEPHONE.

Y y

NAME.

ADDRESS.

TELEPHONE.

NAME.

ADDRESS.

TELEPHONE.

Y y

NAME.

ADDRESS.

TELEPHONE.

NAME.

ADDRESS.

TELEPHONE.

NAME.

ADDRESS.

TELEPHONE.

NAME.

ADDRESS.

       TELEPHONE.

NAME.

ADDRESS.

       TELEPHONE.

NAME.

ADDRESS.

       TELEPHONE.

NAME.

ADDRESS.

       TELEPHONE.

Z z

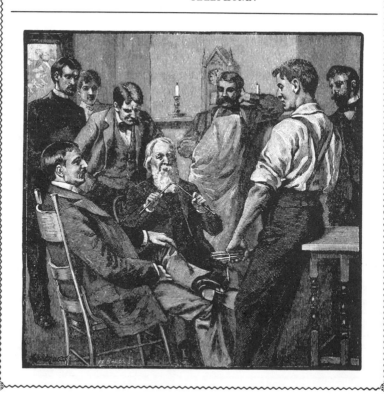

ZEBRA.
zebra.

Z z

NAME.

ADDRESS.

TELEPHONE.

NAME.

ADDRESS.

TELEPHONE.

NAME.

ADDRESS.

TELEPHONE.

NAME.

ADDRESS.

TELEPHONE.

NAME.

ADDRESS.

TELEPHONE.

Z z

NAME.

ADDRESS.

TELEPHONE.

NAME.

ADDRESS.

TELEPHONE.

NAME.

ADDRESS.

TELEPHONE.

NAME.

ADDRESS.

TELEPHONE.

NAME.

ADDRESS.

TELEPHONE.

NAME.

ADDRESS.

TELEPHONE.

Z z

SUNSET.

Now the sun is sinking
In the golden west;
Birds and bees and children
All have gone to rest;

BIRTHDAYS and ANNIVERSARIES.

This book was designed by Jean Callan King/Visuality.

The illustrations were selected from the editions of *McGuffey's Primer* and *First, Second,* and *Third Readers* printed in 1879, 1881, 1885, 1887, 1896, 1907, and 1920.

The type is Scotch Roman and Italic, a style used in several editions of the *McGuffey's Readers* series. It was set on linotype by Pine Tree Composition, Inc., Lewiston, Maine.

The book was printed and bound by Johnson and Hardin, Co., Cincinnati, Ohio. The cover and binding have been adapted from that of the 1879 edition of *McGuffey's Eclectic Readers.*